TIMELESS TALES

Love
Stories

Retold by TANA REIFF
Illustrated by CHERI BLADHOLM

NEW READERS PRESS

Copyright © 1993
New Readers Press
Publishing Division of Laubach Literacy
1320 Jamesville Ave., Syracuse, New York 13210

Printed in the United States of America

9 8 7 6 5

Library of Congress Cataloging-in-Publication Data

Reiff, Tana.
Love stories / retold by Tana Reiff;
illustrated by Cheri Bladholm.
p. cm. — (Timeless tales)
ISBN 0-88336-462-X
1. Readers for new literates. 2. Love stories.
I. Bladholm, Cheri. II. Title. III. Series.
PE1126.A4R444   1993
428.6'2—dc20   93-12038
                                     CIP

Contents

Introduction

Everyone loves a love story. Put together two hearts, and trouble from someone else, and there's probably a good story to be told.

The love stories in this book have been told many times. They have spread from country to country. People have heard some of these stories for thousands of years.

Some love stories are almost the same from one part of the world to another. "Rhodopis and the Golden Shoes" is much like "Cinderella," which almost everyone knows. It is said to be the oldest Cinderella story in the world, and there are many.

Some love stories tell a lot about how people lived. "Test of Fire" and "Deer Hunter and Corn Maiden" both show us tribal ways of life.

Some love stories have happy endings, like the much-loved "Beauty and the Beast" and the very old story, "Cupid and Psyche." Some have very sad endings, like "Romeo and Juliet."

But it doesn't matter how old a story is. Or where it was told. Or how it ends. The reason for a love story is the love in it.

Cupid and Psyche

Ancient Rome

 Back in a time when people believed in gods and goddesses, there lived a very beautiful young woman. Her name was Psyche (SY-key), which means soul.

Word of her great beauty spread, and all the young men came to look at her. They were so taken by Psyche's beauty that they paid no mind to Venus, the goddess of love and beauty. This made Venus very angry.

Now Cupid, the son of Venus, was the god of love. He had great power. By shooting an arrow into any person's heart, Cupid could make that person fall in love. Venus ordered Cupid to make Psyche fall in love with a snake. That way, Venus could win back the hearts of those men who loved only Psyche.

But when Cupid saw Psyche, he too was taken by her beauty. It was as if he had been shot in the heart with his own arrow.

When Venus saw this, she was even more angry. She put a curse on Psyche. She changed Psyche's heart so that she could love no one, and no one could love her.

Psyche's parents asked the gods what they should do. Here was their beautiful daughter, and no man wanted her.

"Dress her in black," the gods said. "Take her to the top of the mountain. Leave her there alone. Her lover will meet her there."

Psyche was afraid. This seemed to be a strange plan. However, she did as the gods said. She waited alone on the mountain to see who would come for her.

The wind, called Zephyr (ZE-fur), saw Psyche waiting there. He blew a soft breeze that lifted Psyche up and away. She rode on the breeze like a bird. Zephyr dropped her in front of a large, fine house.

Psyche stepped inside. Everything in the house was beautiful. But no one was home. There was not a sound. Then Psyche heard voices. "This house is for you," they told her. "We are here to give you anything you need." Psyche didn't see her helpers, or anyone else.

A long table of fine foods was set for her. A warm bath was ready. The sweet music of a harp filled the house. Psyche felt sure her lover would soon be there.

When night came, Psyche lay down in a large bed. The night was very dark. Then, as if by magic, someone was beside her. She could not see him, but he spoke to her.

"I am here for you, if you want me to be," said the man. "But you must never see me. This is how it must be. Will you agree?"

"Yes," said Psyche.

When morning came, the man was gone. But every night he was there, in the dark, never to be seen. He was kind and loving. But Psyche had no idea who he was.

Many nights like this went by. Then one night Psyche decided that she had to see this wonderful person. While he was asleep, she lit an oil lamp. She couldn't believe her eyes. He was the most beautiful man she had ever seen. He had wings on his back. She leaned over for a closer look. As she did, a drop of oil from the lamp fell on him. He woke up with a start.

"You have seen me!" he cried. "You have done a terrible thing! You see, I am Cupid. Now I must leave you. You have broken our trust." With that, Cupid flew off into the night.

Psyche's heart was also broken. "What have I done?" she cried.

Alone in the night, she went over and over in her mind how she might win back Cupid's love. Finally, she decided to pray to Venus, Cupid's mother. This was her only hope.

"I will do anything you ask," Psyche told Venus.

"Very well," said Venus. In the morning, a huge pile of seeds filled the room. There were all kinds—wheat, corn, and flower seeds.

"I want each kind of seed in its own pile," Venus said. "Sort all these seeds by tonight." Then she left the room.

Psyche didn't see how she could ever do this. The pile of seeds was very high. Then, all of a sudden, an army of ants marched into the room. By that night, the ants had sorted all the seeds. The wheat, corn, and flower seeds were each in their own piles.

Venus couldn't believe it. "I'll just have to give you another job," she told Psyche. "Go down to the river. There you will see a flock of golden sheep. They are mean, and strong as lions. Bring me some of their golden wool."

By the time Psyche reached the river, she felt like throwing herself in. How could she ever

get the golden wool from the mean sheep? Just then, a green reed in the river said, "Don't worry. Wait until the sheep walk away. You'll find plenty of their wool left behind on the bushes they pass by."

Psyche did just that. She filled her arms with golden wool. Then she took the wool to Venus.

"I don't believe this!" said Venus. "I will give you yet another job. Take this box down to Hell. Fill the box with beauty. I need it right away."

Psyche did as Venus told her. But on her way back, Psyche again wanted more than she should. She wanted a little of this beauty for herself. Maybe, she hoped, this would win back Cupid's love. So she opened the box just a crack. She saw nothing inside. But the air in the box made her go to sleep.

By this time Cupid was no longer angry.
He only wanted Psyche more than ever. So
he returned. When Psyche woke up, Cupid's
beautiful face was looking at her.

"Come with me!" he said. Together they
went to see Jupiter, the god over all gods and
people. There, on top of Mount Olympus,
Cupid and Psyche were married. As a wedding
present, Jupiter made Psyche a goddess. Now
Venus could no longer be angry with her,
because they both were goddesses.

The wedding of Cupid and Psyche was the
wedding of love and the soul. From that day
on, the two of them—Cupid and Psyche, love
and soul—would always be joined.

Test
of
Fire

New Zealand (Maori)

Beside a blue lake, among large green leaves and bright-colored flowers, lived a beautiful princess named Hine Moa (HI-na MO-a). Her father was chief of the tribe, so many men wanted to marry Hine Moa.

One of these men was a young prince, the chief's son from a tribe across the lake. This was the man that Hine Moa wanted to marry. So he went to Hine Moa's father to ask for her hand. The chief liked the prince at once.

But the match would not be so easy. A mean young man in the tribe also had his eye on Hine Moa. This man, Tai, decided to get rid of the prince.

When night came, Tai sneaked into the chief's storehouse. All the food for the tribe was kept there. When no one was looking, Tai took a bag of potatoes and carried it away. No one saw him, except one old woman.

The next day the chief saw that a bag of potatoes was missing. "Who stole potatoes last night?" he asked.

"I saw the prince from across the lake carrying a bag of potatoes last night," Tai told everyone. The old woman who knew the truth was afraid to speak up.

"To steal from the chief is to steal from the gods," said the chief. "Bring me the prince. He must pay for this!"

The prince was brought before the chief. "Here is what you must do!" the chief told him. "You must walk under the volcano. There is fire there. Everything you pass will make you believe you are in Hell. If you stole the potatoes, you will burn to death. If your heart is pure, you will come out alive."

The prince was afraid. Yet he knew he had not taken the potatoes. So he tried to be brave. Down he went, under the volcano. As he walked, the earth shook. He saw ugly black pools of mud. He passed by rivers of red-hot lava. The fire all around left almost no air. But the prince walked on.

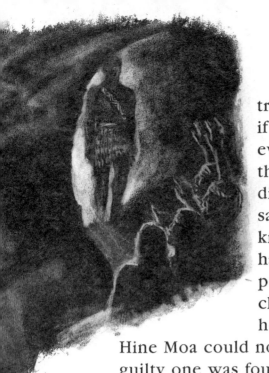

The people of the tribe waited to see if the prince would ever come out of the volcano. He did, and he was safe. Now everyone knew the prince had not taken the potatoes. But the chief sent him home anyway.

Hine Moa could not marry until the guilty one was found.

The prince found life not worth living without Hine Moa. She, too, felt she could not go on. Then one day the prince sent a man to Hine Moa. The man said the prince longed for her. She cried when she heard this.

"Tell the prince I will come to him," said Hine Moa. "Tell him to look for me under the next full moon."

On the night of the full moon, Hine Moa went down to the lake. She looked for a boat to take her across. But her father's men-at-arms stood by all the boats. There was no way she could take one.

There was only one thing to do. Hine Moa jumped into the lake and began to swim.

It was a long way across the lake. Hine Moa swam all night. The water was cold and she grew tired. She stopped to rest when she felt she could not go on. Floating on her back, she looked up. The light of the full moon shone on the lake. The other side was still not in sight.

Somehow, from deep inside her, Hine Moa found the power to go on. As morning came, she spotted land. She pushed on, and at last she dragged herself to shore. The prince was there waiting for her. He took her in his arms. "We are together at last!" he cried.

Just then, the two lovers heard the sound of paddles on the water. The chief's boats were heading in from the lake. Men-at-arms jumped to shore and headed right for Hine Moa and the prince. The lovers ran.

Men-at-arms from the prince's village saw this. They ran toward the lake, ready for war. The young men on both sides were prepared to die.

Back on Hine Moa's side of the lake, the old woman who knew the truth decided it was time to speak. She asked to see the chief. She told him she had seen Tai carry away the bag of potatoes.

The chief leaped into his own boat. He rowed faster than he ever could before. He knew the gods were helping him to reach the other side. They got him there just in time.

"Stop!" the chief cried to his men-at-arms. "Where is your father, the chief?" he asked the prince.

Right then and there, the two chiefs joined the hands of Hine Moa and the prince. The test of their love ended as their life together began.

And what of Tai, the one who really took the potatoes? He had to take the long walk under the volcano. He never came back out into the light of day.

Rhodopis and the Golden Shoes

Egypt

Ra, the sun, rose over the land. Another day began. The morning light showed a young woman on her knees at the Great Sphinx (sfinks). The woman was as lovely as the new day. She was called Rhodopis (ro-DOE-pis), which means rosy-cheeked. She came here every day to greet the sun.

Next she went to the river for a bath. She set down her clothes and her two golden shoes by the river's edge. Then she dipped herself into the water.

All of a sudden Rhodopis heard the flapping of wings above her. She looked up and saw a giant eagle. Before she could do anything, the bird picked up one of her golden shoes. It flew away, holding the shoe in its beak.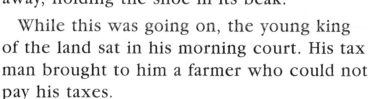

While this was going on, the young king of the land sat in his morning court. His tax man brought to him a farmer who could not pay his taxes.

"I have always paid my taxes," cried the farmer. "But this year birds and rats ate everything I grew. I have nothing left. My wife and children are going hungry! Please, I beg you not to take me away!"

The king was a kind person. It hurt him to hear the poor farmer's story. The king turned to his tax man. "Why did you bring me this man?" the good king asked. "How could I hurt his family more than they are already hurt? Send him home."

The young king said sadly to himself, "That man has no money, but his wife and children make him rich. I, on the other hand, still wait to find a wife."

Just then the king heard the flapping of wings above him. He looked up and saw the giant eagle. The bird dropped from its beak a golden shoe. It landed on the king's lap.

"Look at this shoe," the king said to his court. "It is so small and beautiful." The kind heart of the king told him this was the shoe of a kind-hearted woman. "You must find her," he said to his aide.

Word of the golden shoe went out all over the land. Hundreds of young women lined up in front of the king's temple. Each tried to fit her foot into the tiny shoe. Each one failed.

20

The king's men went out to every little town. Everywhere they went, long lines of women tried on the golden shoe. But no one's foot was small enough to fit.

"This shoe must have an owner somewhere," the king told his aide. "You and I shall set out to find her. We shall first ask the Great Sphinx for help."

So the king and his aide went to the Great Sphinx early in the morning. The sky was still dark. The two watched as Ra came up into the sky. The morning light showed a young woman on her knees. It was Rhodopis greeting the sun as she did every day.

"Young woman!" called the king. "Please come here. Try on this beautiful golden shoe."

Rhodopis did not know this was the king. She wanted to run. But instead she walked over to the two men. She saw that the young man had her lost shoe. She placed a shy foot into it. Of course, it was a perfect fit.

"You are the woman I have been looking for!" cried the king. "Be my wife. Be my queen. We shall be happy together always."

Rhodopis looked into the young man's eyes. They were clear and kind and she loved him right away.

Rhodopis married the king. Together, with kind hearts, they ruled the land for many years.

Beauty and the Beast*

France

Once upon a time, a rich man lost his wife and was left with three daughters. The two older daughters only thought of themselves and who their husbands should be.

The youngest daughter put others before herself. She was beautiful because the heart inside her was so good. Everyone called her Beauty.

---

*There are many versions of this old French folktale. Some say the story was told to help young women accept the fate of arranged marriages to old men.

The family lived in a beautiful house in the city. The father lost all his money, so they moved to a cottage out in the country. The two older daughters moaned and whined about their new life. Beauty, on the other hand, kept a smile on her face. She was happy to cook and clean for the family. At night, she did not long to go to grand balls. Instead, she would read, play the piano, or sing.

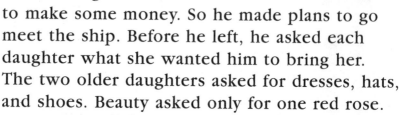

One day, the father heard about a ship coming in. It was full of things that he could sell to make some money. So he made plans to go meet the ship. Before he left, he asked each daughter what she wanted him to bring her. The two older daughters asked for dresses, hats, and shoes. Beauty asked only for one red rose.

As soon as the father made his money, he lost it again. As he headed back to the cottage he ran into a heavy storm. When he believed he could not go on, he saw a light in the gloom. He followed the light, which led him to a fine castle.

He walked inside. A bright fire heated the great dining hall. Dinner was laid out on a long table. But no one came to eat it.

The father waited for hours. At last, he was so hungry that he ate the dinner himself. Then he walked upstairs, found a bedroom, and went to sleep.

The next morning, a big breakfast was laid out for him. Still, he saw no people in the castle.

The father decided to set out on the road again. As he walked down the lane, he picked a rose for Beauty.

All of a sudden he heard a loud voice behind him saying, "You will die for this!" He looked around. He saw a monster, an ugly beast covered with fur.

"The rose is for one of my daughters," said the father.

"Go, then, and send me one of your daughters," said the beast. "If she will die for you, then you may live. Do not betray me, or you will die."

Terrified, the father went back to the cottage. He told his family about the beautiful castle and what the beast had said.

25

"I will die for you,
Father!" Beauty said.
"I would rather die at
the hands of a monster
than of a broken heart
over my father."

And so, three days later, Beauty rode off to
the beast's castle. The two older sisters rubbed
their eyes with onions to make themselves cry.
They didn't really care what happened to their
sweet little sister.

When Beauty saw the beast, she shook all
over. She couldn't believe how ugly he was.

"Did you come here of your own free will?"
the beast asked her.

"Yes."

"That is good," said
the beast.

"Are you going to kill
me now?" asked Beauty.

"Get some sleep first,"
said the beast.

Beauty didn't believe
she could sleep. But as
she did, she had a dream.
A lady came to her. "Your
kindness will be repaid,"
said the lady in the dream.

26

The next morning the beast was nowhere in sight. All alone, Beauty took a look around the castle. To her surprise, she found a door with her name on it. She opened it. The room beyond was full of all her favorite things. The walls were lined with books. There was even a little piano. There was also a sign. It said, "Wish and it will be yours. You are the lady of this house."

All Beauty wanted was to be with her family. She didn't even say that out loud. But as she was thinking it, a large mirror showed her family at the cottage. Her father was crying for her. Her two older sisters wiped away fake tears. They laughed to each other when their father wasn't looking. Beauty cried as well.

That evening a fine dinner was set out for Beauty. As she sat down to eat it, she heard the beast's voice. "May I watch you eat?" he asked.

"This is your house," said Beauty. "Do as you please."

"No, this is your house," said the beast. "You may tell me to go away. Don't you think I'm ugly?"

"Yes," said Beauty. "But when I think of how kind you are, you do not seem so ugly."

"Will you marry me?" the beast asked.

Beauty did not expect to hear this. At first, she couldn't speak. Then she said, "No." That was all.

The beast took a deep breath. It shook the house. "Then good night, Beauty," he said.

The months went by. The beast did not kill Beauty. He was kind to her. During the day she did as she pleased. Each night at dinner the beast came and asked her the same question, "Will you marry me?" And each night Beauty answered, "No."

Even so, she began looking forward to his visits. One night she asked, "Why must you always ask me to marry you? I am your friend. Isn't that enough?"

"Please say you will never leave me," said the beast.

Beauty said nothing, but she did not leave.

One day Beauty saw her father in the magic mirror. He was very sick. "Please," she asked the beast. "May I go and see my father?"

"You may go for eight days," said the beast. "Take this ring. When you are ready to return, leave it on the table."

Beauty went to sleep in the castle that night. The next morning, she woke up in her father's cottage. A chest full of fine clothes was waiting there for her. "The beast must have sent these," she said. "How kind of him."

Beauty's two older sisters came to visit with their new husbands. One husband was good-looking, but his looks were the only thing on his mind. The other was very smart, but he used his brains only to think of mean things to say.

Her sisters didn't like seeing Beauty with the nice clothes from the beast. They decided to get her to stay more than eight days. That way, they hoped Beauty would get into trouble with the beast.

"It's so nice to have you here," said one sister. "Why don't you stay a little longer?"

"We love you so much," said the other.

Beauty was happy to hear such nice words from her sisters. "Perhaps the beast won't mind if I stay a little longer," she said. And so she did.

The night of the tenth day, Beauty had a dream. In it she saw the beast. He lay in the grass by his castle. He looked almost dead.

Beauty woke up with a start. "How could I have stayed away from that dear beast?" she asked herself. "I must get back to him." She laid her ring on the table and fell back to sleep.

When she woke up in the morning, she was in the beast's castle. Right away she went outside. Sure enough, the beast lay in the grass, just like in the dream. "The poor thing!" she screamed. "He is dead! Oh, what have I done?"

She laid her head on the beast's chest. She could hear his heart beating very slowly. "You are alive!" she cried.

Hearing Beauty's voice made the beast feel a little stronger. He began to speak. "You did not come back in eight days," he said. "I was so sad that I began to die."

"Don't die, my dear beast!" cried Beauty. "You must live so I can marry you! I cannot live without you!"

Just as Beauty said that, the castle lit up like the sun. Music rang out. Sparks flew into the sky. And there beside her was not the beast, but a fine-looking young prince!

"Who are you?" she asked the prince.

"It is I, the beast," said the young man. "A fairy put a spell on me. She turned me into a beast. She said I would stay ugly until a young woman would marry me of her own free will. That woman is you, Beauty. Thank you."

Beauty and the prince were married. They had the biggest and best wedding the land had ever seen. He became king and she his queen. And their love stayed strong and true for the rest of their long lives.

Deer Hunter and Corn Maiden

Native American (Tewa)

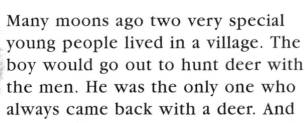

Many moons ago two very special young people lived in a village. The boy would go out to hunt deer with the men. He was the only one who always came back with a deer. And so he was called Deer Hunter. The girl made the pots of clay better than any of the women. She could sew colors onto clothes better than anyone, too. They called her Corn Maiden, a name of honor.

The two young people were the best at what they did. No one was surprised when Deer Hunter and Corn Maiden began spending time together. Everyone knew they were made for each other.

However, before long they began spending too much time together. The people of the village waited for Deer Hunter to bring them deer meat. They became hungry, for Deer Hunter spent all his time with Corn Maiden. She, too, stopped her work. To please the spirit world, everyone was supposed to work. The people were afraid of what the spirit world might do about these two lovers.

Everyone begged Deer Hunter and Corn Maiden to get back to work. But they did not listen. They only drew closer together. Day after day Deer Hunter chased Corn Maiden around the village. They laughed and played always.

Then one day Corn Maiden said she was not feeling well. Three days later she died.

Deer Hunter was sad beyond words. All he did was sit beside Corn Maiden's body. She would be given back to the earth in four days. At that time the people would let her soul go into the spirit world.

On the last day, Deer Hunter began to walk. He roamed out into the fields, far from the village. As the sun was setting, the people were getting ready to give Corn Maiden back to the earth. Deer Hunter kept on walking.

Then he saw a person sitting by a little fire. He walked up and saw that it was Corn Maiden.

She looked as full of life as ever. She was combing her long hair, getting ready to go on to the spirit world.

"Come back with me," begged Deer Hunter.

"I cannot do that," said Corn Maiden. "The spirit world would be angry."

"I will love you forever," Deer Hunter cried to her. "We will always be together."

He tried and tried to talk her into coming back. At last, she said she would.

As they walked into the village, the people were walking in a line. They were heading toward the place where Corn Maiden's soul would be let go. The people were afraid when they saw Corn Maiden. They knew the spirit world did not like it when dead people tried to live again.

Deer Hunter and Corn Maiden tried to start a life together. But in a few days Corn Maiden's face began to look gray. Her skin became dry. In a few more days, there was nothing left of her but skin and bones.

This did not stop the lovers from being together all the time. The people of the village got used to seeing Deer Hunter chase after Corn Maiden just like before.

Then one day, a stranger showed up in the village. He was dressed in white skins. He carried a big bow. Across his back he carried two large arrows.

"I am calling for you," came his voice. "Come out and see me."

Deer Hunter and Corn Maiden knew the spirit world had sent this stranger. They knew he had come for them. So they walked toward him to see what he wanted.

"You want to be together," said the spirit. "Is this so?"

"Yes," said Deer Hunter and Corn Maiden at the same time.

"What you are doing has made the spirit world very angry. And so you will get your wish in the way the spirits choose. You will chase each other across the sky until the end of time. Whenever your people look at the sky, they will remember to live by the old ways. They will remember not to anger the spirit world."

Then the person all in white picked up Deer Hunter, laid him on an arrow, and shot him way up in the sky. With the second arrow, Corn Maiden too was shot into the sky.

That night, and every night after, Deer Hunter and Corn Maiden could be seen as stars in the night sky. One star is very bright, that of the healthy young man. The other star is dim, that of the woman who faded away after death. They will chase each other across the sky forever.

Introduction to
"Romeo
and
Juliet"

This story was made famous by the great English playwright, William Shakespeare. However, it is an old Italian story. This version is adapted from one of the Italian tellings, by Matteo Bandello. We use the names Montague (MON-ta-gew) and Capulet, though, as in the Shakespeare version. Also, the story here is divided into sections that roughly match the five acts of Shakespeare's play.

Romeo
and
Juliet

Italy

In the city of Verona, many years
ago, there lived two families who did
not get along. The hate between the
Capulet family and the Montague
family went so far back that no one knew
the reason anymore.

One time the Capulet family had a big
party. Of course, they did not invite anyone
named Montague. However, Romeo Montague
heard about the party. He decided to go along
with some other young men. Romeo and his
friends wore party masks, and no one knew
who they were.

After dinner, Romeo took off his mask. He looked around the room. Right away his eyes caught those of pretty young Juliet Capulet. Neither knew who the other was. Each would look away, then back again, only to catch the other watching.

At last Romeo sat down next to Juliet. One of his friends sat on her other side. The friend took her right hand in his. "Your hand is cold," said the friend.

"My hands are always cold," said Juliet.

Romeo took her left hand. "This hand is warm," he said. Juliet was surprised, and her sweet face changed color as they spoke.

When it was time to leave, Romeo asked his friend, "Who was that woman?"

"Do you not know?" laughed the friend. "That was Juliet Capulet!"

"Surely you are joking!" said Romeo. "I did not know the Capulets had such a lovely daughter. This could be a problem, my friend. I am already in love with her."

After the party Juliet asked her mother, "Who was that young man?"

"That was Romeo Montague," said Juliet's mother. "You must stay away from him."

"I do not believe such a nice man could be any harm," said Juliet.

"It does not matter," said her mother. "He is a Montague."

2

That night Juliet did not sleep. All she could think about was Romeo. She went to her window. Everything outside was quiet until she heard the sound of someone walking. She said to herself, "Can it be? Yes, it is Romeo! But why?"

Then she called down to Romeo, "What are you doing at this house, Montague? How did you find my window? My family will kill you if they find you here!"

"I have come to tell you I am yours forever," said Romeo, "if you will have me. Love brought me. And I hope our love can bring our families together."

"I am yours as well, dear Romeo," said Juliet. "But you must go."

"I will go now," said Romeo. "But I will return!" With that, he blew her a kiss. Then he was gone.

Just then, Juliet's nurse came into her room. "Who are you talking to?" the old woman asked.

"Oh, dear lady, it was Romeo of the Montague family," cried Juliet. "What am I to do about this love?"

"Love cannot be killed," said the nurse. "I will help you in any way I can."

"Please talk to Romeo," Juliet begged. "See about a way for us to marry."

In this city there was a man of the church named Friar Lawrence. Everyone in Verona knew and loved him. Romeo went to Friar Lawrence to tell him about Juliet.

"I would rather die than break a promise of the heart," said Romeo. "We must be married. But how?"

"Perhaps if you and Juliet married, your two families would come together," said Friar Lawrence. "I am willing to marry you in secret. Make a rope ladder. You will need it."

Juliet's nurse came to speak with Romeo. He told her the plan to meet at the church. "And here, take this rope ladder which I have made. Give it to Juliet. Tell her to hide it in her room."

3

The next Saturday, Romeo and Juliet were married. Juliet went back to her house and waited in her room. She watched out her window for Romeo to show up. Every minute of waiting seemed like a thousand years.

Then he was there. Juliet let down the rope ladder. Romeo climbed up and into her room through the window.

They kissed and held each other as if they could never let go. "Oh, my love, my love," cried Juliet.

"We are husband and wife now," said Romeo. "I am so very happy."

The room was lit with candles. Love filled every space. Romeo stayed until the first light of morning. Every night he returned, only to climb down before the sun came up.

Not long after, the fight between the two families got much worse. There was a battle, the worst ever. When it was over, Romeo had killed Juliet's cousin Tybalt (TI-balt).

The court ordered Romeo to leave Verona forever. He had no choice but to go to another city.

Juliet cried day and night. Her family believed she was crying for Tybalt. They still did not know that their daughter was married.

"What is wrong with this girl?" her father asked her mother. "She should not still be crying over her cousin."

"I think she needs a husband," said her mother. "It is time for you to find her one."

In a few days, everything was set. Juliet would marry a young man named Paris. But when her parents told her the news, she only cried more.

"I will die before I marry that man!" Juliet said.

"You will marry Paris or you are out of this family," said her father. "That is the end of it."

4

 The first chance she got, Juliet went to visit Friar Lawrence. "What can I do?" she cried to him. "I cannot marry Paris, because I am already married to Romeo."

At first, Friar Lawrence said nothing. He was thinking about what to do. Then he walked into a back room. He came back with a tiny bottle in his hand.

"This is a very special drug," he explained to Juliet. "Drink it the night before your wedding. You will fall into a deep sleep. Even the best doctor in Verona will believe you are dead. But the drug lasts for only two days. I will send word to Romeo. He will come and open your grave. You will wake up. Then you and he can go and start a life together."

"This is a fine plan!" said Juliet. For the first time in weeks, she felt happy. She danced all the way home, light as air.

The night before the wedding, Juliet took out the tiny bottle. As she looked at it, she began to worry. "What if I never wake up?" she wondered. "Or what if I wake up in my grave before Romeo gets there? What if bugs and worms come to eat my body?"

Then she stopped thinking and drank the drug all at once.

The morning of the wedding, Juliet's nurse came to wake her. "You sleep too long!" said the old woman. "This is your wedding day!" But Juliet did not move. The nurse shook her, but Juliet was cold as stone.

"Oh, my dear girl!" sobbed the nurse. "You have died before your wedding, as you said you would."

Friar Lawrence wrote a note to Romeo. But some of the friars were very sick. No one could enter or leave the church to take the note to him. So Romeo did not hear about the secret plan.

Juliet's family was very, very sad. They laid her to rest in the family grave. Everyone said goodbye to her.

5

Word of Juliet's death reached Romeo. Then and there he decided to end his own life. He did not want to live without Juliet.

Romeo headed back to Verona. On the way, he stopped to buy some poison. He reached the city at night and went to Juliet's grave. He opened it up, and there she was. Her face was as sweet as ever. Her lips were cold as he kissed them for the last time. Then he took the poison and fell dead upon his one true love.

Romeo's falling woke Juliet. She screamed when she saw that Romeo was dead. Then she began to sob, and her tears fell on his chest.

Just then, Juliet saw Romeo's dagger, still with him. She pulled it out, and without waiting even for a second, Juliet stabbed herself in the heart. Before, she had faked death. Now she was truly dead.

And so ends this old story of tragic love. Friar Lawrence was taken to court for his part in this sad matter, and then set free. The man who sold Romeo the poison was hanged. Juliet's nurse was ordered to leave Verona. And the families of Capulet and Montague forgot their hate, and never fought again. In this way the love between Romeo and Juliet lived on.